Sew Mini GARDENS

More Than 18 Plant Plushies to Stitch & Stuff

by the editors of Klutz

KLUTZ®

CONTENTS

Look for the color bar on the side of the page to jump right to the garden you want to make.

DESERT GARDEN

PEACE GARDEN

HUNGRY GARDEN

FLOWER GARDEN

DESERT GARDEN

Nice to meet you!

What YOU GET

10 colors of felt

Tray

Pot

5 pipe cleaners

Stuffing

5 colors of embroidery floss

Traceable patterns

30 pre-cut eyes

30 pre-cut cheeks

2 needles with holder

Other stuff you need:

Scissors (small, sharp blades are best)
Fingernail clippers
Fine-tipped marker or ink pen

Optional:

Thimble • Thin wire
Chopsticks or a pencil

GARDEN CONTAINERS

A garden is a friend you can visit any time. Give your friends a nice home.

For stemmed plants, bend the base of the stem (pipe cleaner) around the inside of the pot until the plant can stand on its own.

Use the included pot for any single plants looking for love.

Use the planter for any plant who has sprouted roots and made a family.

MORE IDEAS FROM HOME
Look around your house for items to add to your garden.

DECORATE YOUR DISH

Keep the containers white for a modern style or try decorating them. You can make designs with:

permanent markers

stickers

other craft supplies

STYLISH SOIL

Landscape your garden with different types of ground coverings:

fish tank gravel

moss

sand

CREATIVE CONTAINERS

Make more containers from things found in your home:

- **empty (and cleaned) soup or veggie cans**
- **mint tins**
- **coffee mugs**
- **old saucers or small plates**
- **small ceramic pots**
- **glass bud vases**

This bunch loves to have fun under the sun!

DESERT GARDEN

SAGUARO CACTUS

The saguaro cactus is happy and huggable, and a great first project for your training as a mini gardener!

You can call me "Suh-wah-row."

Every project in this book comes with a garden guide, which shows how many colors of floss and felt pieces you need.

Also, keep the eyes, cheeks, stuffing, and needle, plus a pen and pair of scissors (from home) handy. You will need those for almost every project.

GARDEN GUIDE

DESERT ZONE

4 FLOSS COLORS
black, white, pink, and green

3 FELT PIECES

x2

2 saguaro cactus bodies

1 saguaro cactus bottom

BRIGHT IDEA

You don't have to match the colors of the projects in the photos—plant your own ideas!

8

Tracing and Cutting
PATTERNS

You will need:
- Ballpoint pen or thin marker to trace on the felt
- Sharp, small scissors to cut the felt in clean lines.

1 Place the saguaro cactus pattern on top of a piece of felt. Line it up very close to the edges to get the most out of the felt without wasting too much. (See the pattern guide in the box.)

2 With a pen, trace around the pattern.

3 Place the cactus pattern on the felt again, very close to the first one you traced. Trace the pattern again. Then trace the cactus bottom.

4 Using sharp scissors, very carefully cut along the lines you've traced on the felt. When you're done, one side might have lines or marks from tracing on it. That's now called the "wrong side" of the felt. Wrong sides always end up on the inside, so you won't see them.

Go slowly and watch your fingers.

You can set the patterns aside for now.

9

USING FLOSS

Embroidery floss usually has six thin strands wound together. For the projects in this book, you'll only need two strands. Here's how to separate them.

USE ONE THREAD FOR SEWING PATTERNS TOGETHER

1 Remove the rubber band from the bundle of floss you want to use, and unwind about 14 inches (35.5 cm). Cut it off.

2 Hold the floss gently in one hand, about 1 inch (2.5 cm) from the end.

3 With your other hand, pull one strand of floss up . . .

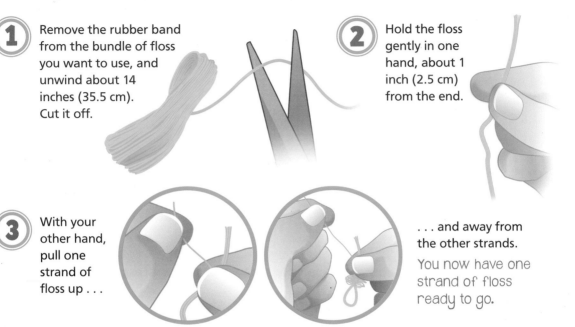

. . . and away from the other strands.

You now have one strand of floss ready to go.

USE TWO THREADS FOR SEWING FACES AND DETAILS

1 Repeat Steps 2–3.

2 Take your two separated strands of floss, smooth them out, and line them up together.

⚙ BRIGHT IDEA
Keep your spare strands of floss loose and untangled, so you can use them later for another project.

Threading
THE NEEDLE

☀ BRIGHT IDEA

You may need to trim the end of the floss first, if it's frayed or bent.

1 Moisten one end and pinch the strands together so they're nice and pointy.

2 Poke the pointy end through the hole in the needle (this is called the eye).

3 Pull the strand until the two ends of the floss are even lengths.

Do Steps 1-3 with two strands of thread if you are getting ready to sew a face or details.

SAFETY ✕ STUFF

- Always handle needles with care. Don't rush the stitches.

- Needles are sharp. If you have a thimble, wear it to protect your fingertips while stitching.

- Keep needles away from small children, pets, and bare feet.

- Store your needles when you're finished working. You can use the needle holder provided, or a storage unit of your choice.

- If a needle breaks, carefully check the surrounding area and throw out broken needle pieces.

- If a needle breaks the skin, gently clean the area and apply a bandage. Get an adult to help you.

- These plants are for decoration only. Do not give them to small children to play with.

- If finished projects get dirty, spot-clean them with a damp rag and warm water. Do not wash the felt in a washing machine.

- Supplies included should only be used for the projects in this book.

Tying a
STARTING KNOT

This is also called a "French knot."

1 Hold the threaded needle in one hand and the ends of the floss in the other. Place them under the needle and flat against the side of your finger to hold them in place.

2 Then wrap the long end of the floss up and around the needle three or four times.

Don't let the ends of the floss slip from under the needle as you wrap.

3 Move your thumb up to hold the wrapped floss in place, then let go of the long end of floss.

4 Hold the wrapped thread with one hand, and the needle with the other hand. Carefully slide the wrapped thread down the needle, all the way to the end of the floss.

Do Steps 1-4 with a threaded needle that has two strands for faces and details.

It should tie a knot right near the end of your strand.

BRIGHT IDEA
If you are having trouble mastering the French knot, any knot you tie near the end of the strand will work just fine.

MAKE A FACE

Bring your desert plant to life with eyes and cheeks.

Eyes &
CHEEKS

Start with the eyes. They'll help guide where the rest of the face should go.

1 Place the eyes on the front of the cactus, just below its shoulders. The wrong side should be facing down.

2 Using a needle with black floss, poke up through the back of your felt and through the eye.

3 Poke your needle back through the other side of the eye and finish your floss (page 15). Repeat Steps 2–3 to attach the second eye.

4 Use white floss to make two small stitches in the middle of each eye to brighten them up!

5 Attach the cheeks the same way, with pink floss and one small stitch each.

13

MOUTH

How to Back Stitch

Use "back stitch" to make a line without gaps. Your plant will sprout a smile!

 Poke your needle through from the underside of your felt. Pull until the starting knot just touches the back of the felt, then poke the needle back through the felt to make one tiny stitch.

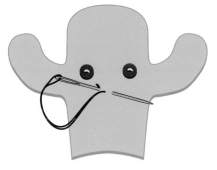

 Poke your needle through the bottom again, one stitch length away from your first stitch.

 Now you'll do something a little different: Poke your needle into the ending hole of your last stitch, then poke it back up one stitch length past your starting point.

 Pull your floss all the way through until it lies flat without puckering. That's one back stitch!

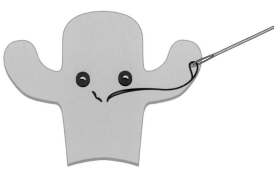

5 Repeat Steps 3–4 until you reach the end of the mouth. Poke back through the felt one more time, then finish your floss (page 15).

ENDING KNOT

Don't let your floss fly away! Make a knot so your stitches stay strong.

ENDING KNOTS FOR FACES AND DETAILS

 Turn the felt over so that you're looking at the wrong side. Poke the needle under one of the nearby stitches (not through the felt) to create a loop.

 Slide the needle through the loop and pull until you have a knot close to the felt.

3 Repeat Steps 1–2 to make an extra strong knot. Then trim the thread close to the felt.

ENDING KNOTS FOR SEWING PATTERNS TOGETHER

 After you make your last stitch, poke through both pieces of felt to make an additional loop.

 Slide the needle through the loop and pull until you've made a knot close to the felt.

 Repeat Steps 1–2 to make an extra strong knot. Then trim the thread close to the felt.

DETAILS

Give your plant some flair before you sew it together!

LINES

1 With a pen, make little dots as guides to keep your lines straight.

2 Use back stitch to make lines (page 14).

Free hugs!

SPINES

You can use scraps of thread to make spines.

1 Thread a needle, but don't add a starting knot. Leave the thread hanging loose.

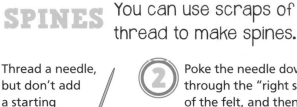

2 Poke the needle down through the "right side" of the felt, and then back up, making a small stitch. Leave a tiny tail of floss.

3 Carefully poke the needle back down near the floss tail.

4 Bring the needle back up through the felt near the stitch. Snip the floss ½ inch (13 mm) from the felt, so that you have a second floss tail.

5 Repeat Steps 1–4 all over the cactus. When you are happy with the number of spines, finish by trimming them all the same length.

SEW TOGETHER
How to Whip Stitch

1 Lay the "wrong" sides of the two cactus bodies together.

Start at the bottom edge of the cactus. Poke the needle through the top piece of felt to hide the knot.

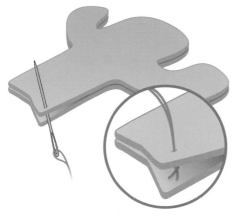

2 Loop the thread around and poke the needle up through both layers of the felt to make one whip stitch.

Now make another stitch through both layers of felt.

3 Keep stitching this way all the way around until you reach the bottom corner on the other side.

4 Finish your floss (page 15).

Cactus makes perfect!

HOW TO STUFF

(5) Pinch off a small amount of the stuffing (a little goes a long way) and push it into the area of the cactus you've just sewn. It's easier if you roll the stuffing in your fingers first.

☀ BRIGHT IDEA

Use a chopstick or a pencil to push stuffing into hard-to-reach parts of your plants (like the saguaro cactus's arms).

ADD THE BOTTOM

(6) Place the cactus bottom circle against the base of the cactus, with the "wrong" side facing in.

(7) Starting at the back of the cactus, use a whip stitch to attach the bottom to the cactus.

(8) Whip stitch all the way around so there is no gap. Then finish with an ending knot (page 15).

HI!

Wave hello to your finished saguaro!

MORE DETAILS

Hot accessories make your cactus look cool.

> You're stuck with me.

FRINGY FLOWERS

Use this pattern

2½"

¾"

Any skinny rectangle scrap will work!

1 Snip little fringes along one edge. (Don't cut all the way through!)

2 Roll the fringe up like a cinnamon bun.

3 With a threaded needle, poke through the layers at the bottom so the roll holds tight.

4 Stitch the flower to the arms or the top of the cactus.

FLOWERS

Use this pattern

1 Attach the flower to the cactus with a few stitches through the center of the flower.

I am also known as a prickly pear.

PADDLE CACTUS

GARDEN GUIDE

DESERT ZONE

4 FLOSS COLORS
black, white, pink, and blue

8 FELT PIECES

x3 — 3 paddle cactus bodies

1 paddle cactus bottom

x2 — 2 buds

2 forked bud*

*Trace the forked buds the opposite way, so the final pieces mirror each other.

MAKE A FACE

1 Add a face to one of the paddle cactus pieces (pages 13–14). Put it slightly above the center.

☼ BRIGHT IDEA
Now is a great time to add spines or other details to all the paddle cactus pieces.

SEW TOGETHER

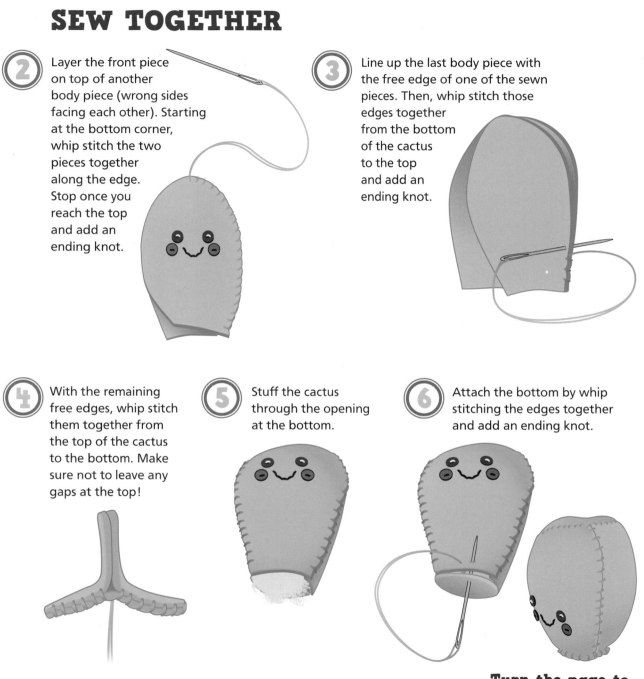

2 Layer the front piece on top of another body piece (wrong sides facing each other). Starting at the bottom corner, whip stitch the two pieces together along the edge. Stop once you reach the top and add an ending knot.

3 Line up the last body piece with the free edge of one of the sewn pieces. Then, whip stitch those edges together from the bottom of the cactus to the top and add an ending knot.

4 With the remaining free edges, whip stitch them together from the top of the cactus to the bottom. Make sure not to leave any gaps at the top!

5 Stuff the cactus through the opening at the bottom.

6 Attach the bottom by whip stitching the edges together and add an ending knot.

Turn the page to add the buds.

MAKE BUDS

Don't call them leaves! Buds are actually the cactus version of branches. In fact, if you take a bud and plant it in the ground, it will grow into a new cactus!

7 With the wrong sides together, whip stitch the buds, leaving a small gap.

8 Stuff the bud and whip stitch the bottom to close it. Finish the floss (page 15).

9 Repeat Steps 7–8 with the other bud.

10 Whip stitch the bottom of the buds onto the seam closest to the face.

Buds are in charge of making the cactus flowers. Decorate your cactus with flowers and bring on the bloom!

Try one bud.

Or two of the same pattern.

Spiky and sweet!

22

GARDEN GUIDE

 DESERT ZONE

1 FLOSS COLOR
any colored thread

✂ **1 FELT PIECE**

1 button cactus

BUTTON CACTUS

1 With the felt circle lying flat, poke a threaded needle about ⅛ inch (3 mm) from the edge. Make sure you have a sturdy starting knot (page 12).

2 Make straight stitches all the way around the circle, following the edge of the circle.

3 Pull the thread tight until the circle bunches up and makes a little pocket. Fill it with stuffing and pull the thread tightly so the opening closes up.

☼ **BRIGHT IDEA**
This technique is called gathering. Keep an eye out for it when you make the spider on page 43!

4 Poke the needle all the way through the cactus, from bottom to top. Bring the needle and thread around the side of the cactus to the base, and back through the same spot.

 5 This time, pull the needle and thread around the side opposite your last stitch.

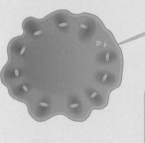

Repeat about eight times. Finish your floss (page 15).

Ta-da! Cute as a button!

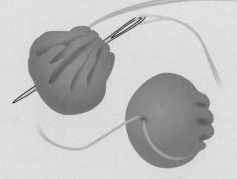

GARDEN GUIDE

🌵 DESERT FRIEND

🧵 3 FLOSS COLORS
black, white, and pink

✂️ 4 FELT PIECES

x2

2 fennec fox bodies

1 fennec fox muzzle

1 fennec fox tail

FENNEC FOX

Your plants will love their new fox friend!

Three cheers for big ears!

MAKE A FACE

1 Attach the muzzle, with a back stitched nose (page 14).

2 Add eyes and cheeks on either side of the muzzle.

3 Back stitch the ear lines using hot pink floss.

ADD A TAIL

4 Stitch the base of the tail to the corner of the other body piece (the one without the face), as shown. Secure with an end knot.

SEW TOGETHER

5 Stack the two body pieces, wrong sides together. Whip stitch them together, leaving a gap at the bottom.

6 Stuff the body and whip stitch the gap closed. Finish the floss (page 15).

PEACE GARDEN

Grow your own paradise!

ECHEVERIA SUCCULENT

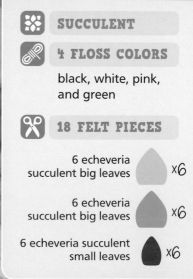

GARDEN GUIDE

SUCCULENT

4 FLOSS COLORS

black, white, pink, and green

18 FELT PIECES

6 echeveria succulent big leaves x6

6 echeveria succulent big leaves x6

6 echeveria succulent small leaves x6

MAKE A FACE

1 Add a face to one of the big light green leaves (pages 13-14).

MAKE A SEAM

Gather all the big dark green leaves, including the leaf with a face.

2 Fold one of the big leaves in half lengthwise.

3 Whip stitch just the bottom edges together to make a seam. Secure it with an ending knot (page 15).

4 Then, do the same with the other big leaves.

MAKE LEAF LAYERS ◇◇◇◇◇◇◇◇◇◇◇

5 Poke your needle through the bottom of one of the big leaves, stringing it on the thread like a bead.

6 String the remaining big leaves. Push them together so there is no gap in between leaves.

7 Next, poke your needle through the bottom of the first leaf again.

8 Then, pull the thread tight, until the leaves form a flower shape. Secure the leaf layer with an ending knot (page 15).

9 Repeat Steps 2–8 with the other big leaves and the small leaves.

SEW TOGETHER

10 Start with the dark green layer first. Poke your threaded needle up through the bottom of the felt.

11 Next, stack the bright green layer on top and poke the needle up through the center.

12 Then, stack the pink layer on top and poke the needle through the center.

13 Attach the layers together by poking the needle back down through all the layers of felt and pulling the thread tight. Secure with an ending knot (page 15) on the underside of the bottom layer.

Petal to the metal!

ALOE VERA

GARDEN GUIDE

⊞ **SUCCULENT**

✄ **4 FLOSS COLORS**

black, white, pink, and green

✄ **11 FELT PIECES**

x5   1 aloe vera base   x5

5 aloe vera outer leaves   5 aloe vera inner leaves

MAKE A FACE

1 Add a face to one of the aloe vera outer leaf pieces.

② MAKE DARTS

Each outer piece has a little cutout triangle.

Fold one in half lengthwise.

Whip stitch the cutout triangles, edges together to make a dart. Secure with an ending knot (page 15).

Darts help make rounder shapes when sewing.

Then, do the same with the other outer leaves.

Each inner piece has two long edges and two short edges.

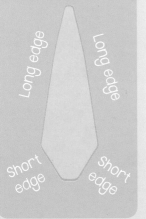

MAKE ALOE LEAVES

③ Stack one inner piece inside an outer piece. Line up the tips.

The inner piece will be shorter than the outer piece.

Whip stitch the long edges together, beginning and ending above the dart.

Repeat with the other leaves.

SEW TOGETHER

4 Take two of the leaves, and hold them so their "right" sides are together. Whip stitch the short yellow edges together. Secure with an end knot.

Outer piece

Stitch the yellow felt, not the green.

It should look like this.

5 Repeat Step 4 with the remaining open edges until they are all sewn together in a circle.

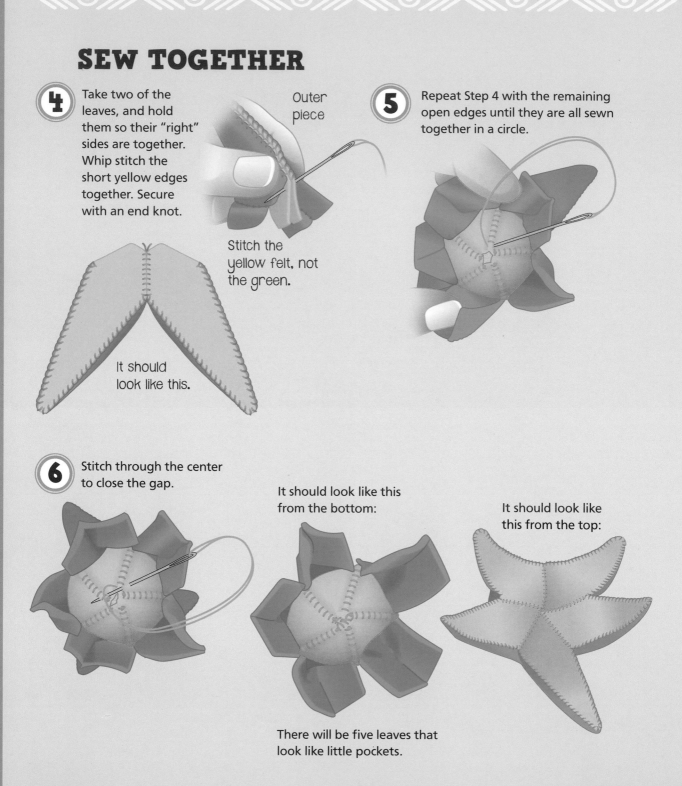

6 Stitch through the center to close the gap.

It should look like this from the bottom:

It should look like this from the top:

There will be five leaves that look like little pockets.

Stuff all five leaves. Add stuffing until it reaches the unsewn edges. You will stuff more before you finish.

 Stuffing a little now helps fan out the leaves and makes it easier to finish the project.

 Line up the free edges of two outer (green) pieces and whip stitch them together. Secure with an ending knot.

It should look like this.

9 Add more stuffing to fill in the bottom of the leaves.

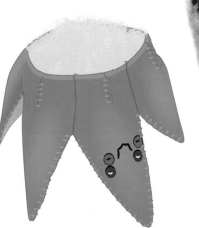

10 Whip stitch the aloe's base to the bottom of the leaves. Finish with an ending knot.

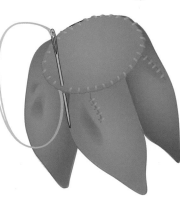

Aloe there!

ROSETTE SUCCULENT

GARDEN GUIDE

- **SUCCULENT**
- **1 FLOSS COLOR**
  green
- **1 FELT PIECE**

1 rosette succulent

TRACING TIP:

There are little dots on the pattern. Make sure to make a mark in each hole. This mark is where you stop cutting each petal.

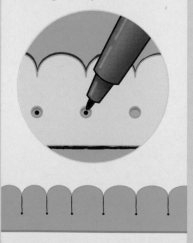

1 Tightly roll up the succulent shape, starting from the smaller petals.

The straight edge will be the base.

2 To secure the roll, poke a threaded needle through all the layers at the base of the succulent. Pull the thread tight and poke the needle back through all the layers again.

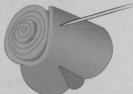

3 Keep turning the roll and continue to poke through all the layers at the base until the succulent stays rolled, then secure with an ending knot (page 15).

Be mindful of where you poke and don't hit your finger!

4 Peel back the petals to make the succulent bloom!

YOGA FROG

MAKE A FACE

1 Back stitch the closed eyes with black floss and the mouth and nose with green floss.

SEW TOGETHER

2 Stack the two body pieces (wrong sides facing). Whip stitch them together, leaving a small gap at the bottom.

3 Stuff the body and whip stitch the gap closed. Secure with an ending knot (page 15).

GARDEN GUIDE

- **PEACEFUL FRIEND**
- **3 FLOSS COLORS**
  black, green, and blue
- **6 FELT PIECES**

x2
2 yoga frog bodies

x2
2 yoga frog legs

x2
2 yoga frog arms

4 Place an arm on the back of the body, just below the neck. Attach with just one stitch.

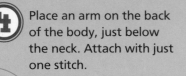

5 Then, push the threaded needle through the frog's body to the opposite side and attach the other arm. Secure the arms with an ending knot.

6 Make a small stitch through the hands and finish the floss.

7 Attach each leg to the front of the body with one stitch and secure it with an ending knot.

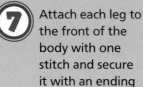

Ohm ... ribbit, ribbit!

8 Crisscross the legs. Make a small stitch from the back through the feet and the body. Secure with an ending knot.

These plants
are carnivorous!
That means they
eat insects and
other critters.

HUNGRY GARDEN

VENUS FLYTRAP

MAKE A FACE

① Add a pair of eyes on one of the Venus flytrap heads. (pages 13–14). Put the eyes slightly toward the bottom, away from the dart.

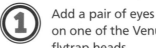

SEW TOGETHER

② Whip stitch the dart (page 31). This will be the back of the head.

③ Next, whip stitch the mouth and head pieces together, placing the teeth between the layers as you stitch across the front.

Leave a small gap at the back after you finish stitching the teeth.

GARDEN GUIDE

CARNIVOROUS

3 FLOSS COLORS
black, white, and green

4 FELT PIECES

x2

2 Venus flytrap heads

x2

2 Venus flytrap mouths

scraps of white felt to make teeth

 1 STEM
half a pipe cleaner

☼ BRIGHT IDEA
Add as many or as few teeth as you want. Eight teeth is a mouthful, but one tooth still makes a statement.

4 Stuff the mouth and whip stitch the gap closed. Finish it with an ending knot (page 15).

TOP VIEW
This will be the top of the flytrap.

5 Repeat Steps 2–4 with the other head, mouth, and teeth.

This will be the bottom of the flytrap.

6 Whip stitch the top and bottom together at the back.

Try to line up the darts.

ADD A STEM

7 Fold a pipe cleaner in half and cut it with a fingernail clipper. Use one half for a stem and put the other piece aside to use later.

8 Hold the pipe cleaner on the back of the plant. Poke a threaded needle through the plant. Whip stitch over the pipe cleaner. Then go back through the plant. Repeat a few times, then finish with an ending knot.

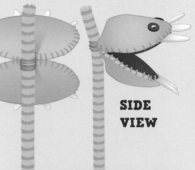

SIDE VIEW

☼ BRIGHT IDEA

Leave a little bit of the pipe cleaner sticking up above the whip stitches.

9 Fold the top bit of the pipe cleaner down, over the stitches.

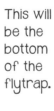

Munch, munch! Ready for lunch!

PITCHER PLANT

MAKE A FACE

1 Add a face on one of the pitchers (pages 13–14) at the widest part.

SEW TOGETHER

2 Stack the two pitchers with wrong sides facing in, and whip stitch them together, leaving the top edge free. Finish it with an ending knot (page 15).

3 Stuff only the bottom of the pitcher plant.

4 Using a pencil or your fingertips, tuck in the top edges.

Don't sew the top closed.

5 Flip the plant over and whip stitch the leaf onto the back near the top.

6 Turn the plant, so the leaf is pointing down. Add a stem (page 39).

Flip the plant face up. Bend the pipe cleaner down until the pitcher looks like it's hanging.

GARDEN GUIDE

- **CARNIVOROUS**
- **4 FLOSS COLORS**
  black, white, pink, and green
- **3 FELT PIECES**
  x2
  2 pitcher plant   1 pitcher plant leaf
- **1 STEM**
  half a pipe cleaner

ENCHANTRESS PLANT

These plants really don't exsist, but it shouldn't stop you from bringing them to life.

MAKE A FACE

1 Add a pair of eyes to one of the plant pieces (pages 13–14). Put them slightly above the skinny part, as shown.

SEW TOGETHER

2 Repeat Steps 2–4 from the Pitcher Plant (page 40).

Just try to resist our charms!

3 Whip stitch the rose petal to the back of the plant with a few stitches and finish it with an ending knot (page 15).

BACK VIEW

FRONT VIEW

4 Add a stem (page 39).

GARDEN GUIDE

 **CARNIVOROUS**

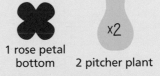 **4 FLOSS COLORS**

black, white, pink, and teal

3 FELT PIECES

1 rose petal bottom   2 pitcher plant x2

1 STEM

half a pipe cleaner

TUBE PLANTS

These are another type of pitcher plant, which catch bugs in their tubes.

1 Fold one tube and whip stitch along the long edge. Finish it with an ending knot (page 15).

2 Repeat Step 1 with the other two tubes.

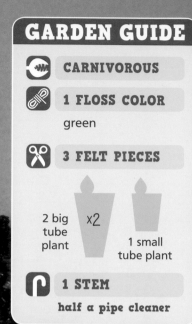

GARDEN GUIDE

🌀 **CARNIVOROUS**

🧵 **1 FLOSS COLOR**
green

✂️ **3 FELT PIECES**

2 big tube plant   x2   1 small tube plant

🔁 **1 STEM**
half a pipe cleaner

3 Hold the bottoms of the tubes together. Stitch them together and tie an ending knot.

4 Wrap a pipe cleaner around the bottom of the group. Trim the pipe cleaner to fit.

Like this:

5 Whip stitch through the tubes and around the pipe cleaner all the way around. Secure with an ending knot.

⚙️ **BRIGHT IDEA**
Mix and match long and short tubes however you like. Bugs beware!

SPIDER

MAKE A FACE

 1 With white and pink floss, back stitch eyes and a mouth on the body.

GARDEN GUIDE

HUNGRY FRIEND

3 FLOSS COLORS

white, pink, and black

2 FELT PIECES

1 spider body 1 spider legs

You can find this same gathering technique with the button cactus (page 23), too!

SEW TOGETHER

 2 Flip the body so the wrong side is facing you. With a threaded needle, make a knot on the edge of the circle.

3 With black floss, make straight stitches all the way around the circle to gather the edge.

4 Pull the thread so the edges will bunch up and make a little pocket. Fill it with stuffing and pull the thread tightly to close the gap. Finish it with an ending knot.

This is the spider's body!

HURRY! TURN THE PAGE SO I CAN HAVE LEGS TO ESCAPE THIS HUNGRY GARDEN!

5 Attach the spider's legs by poking the threaded needle through the bottom of the body, then through the center of the legs.

6 Poke back up through the legs and into the head again. Repeat until it feels secure, and finish.

Let's hang out!

Rest the spider next to a plant or sew it onto one of the plant stems.

FLY

MAKE A FACE

1 Back stitch a pair of eyes to the center of the fly's body.

GARDEN GUIDE

 HUNGRY FRIEND

 3 FLOSS COLORS
green, black, and white

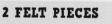 **2 FELT PIECES**

1 fly   1 cactus flower

To make wings, cut a heart shape from the cactus flower.

SEW TOGETHER

2 Follow page 43 (Steps 2-4) to make the body, but don't use any stuffing.

This is the fly's body!

3 Attach the fly's wings by stitching through the fly's body and the wings. Repeat a few times and finish.

LET'S FLY! To make the fly hover, poke a thin wire or an unfolded paper clip from home through the body.

Stem-sational!

FLOWER GARDEN

GARDEN GUIDE

 FLOWER

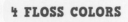 **4 FLOSS COLORS**

black, white, pink, and yellow

✂ **3 FELT PIECES**

x2 2 daisy centers

1 daisy petals

🌱 **1 STEM**

half a pipe cleaner

See page 34 for tips on tracing the daisy petals.

DAISY
SEW TOGETHER

MAKE A FACE

1 Add a face to one of the daisy centers.

2 Stack the face on the other center, with the wrong sides facing each other. Whip stitch them together, leaving a small gap.

3 Stuff and whip stitch the gap closed. Finish with an ending knot.

4 With a threaded needle, make large straight stitches all the way across the straight edge of the petal piece. Then remove the needle, but DO NOT add an end knot yet!

5 Pull the floss tight like a drawstring to make a petal ring.

6 With the daisy center lying facedown, place the petal ring on top.

Tighten or loosen the petal ring so it's a tiny bit smaller than the outside edge of the daisy center.

7 Whip stitch the bottom of the ring onto the back of the circle.

8 Attach the stem to the back of the flower (page 39).

WILD FLOWER

MAKE A FACE

1 Add a face to one of the daisy centers.

SEW TOGETHER

2 Start to whip stitch the face to the wildflower petals, but stop about halfway around.

3 Add a tiny bit of stuffing before you finish stitching and add an end knot.

4 Attach the stem to the back of the flower (page 39).

Stitch a leaf to any of your garden flower's stems.

GARDEN GUIDE

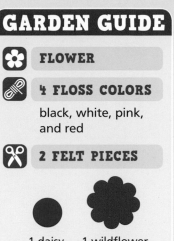

❁ **FLOWER**

🧵 **4 FLOSS COLORS**
black, white, pink, and red

✂ **2 FELT PIECES**

1 daisy center

1 wildflower petals

🔩 **1 STEM**
half a pipe cleaner

ROSE

GARDEN GUIDE

❀ **FLOWER**

🧵 **4 FLOSS COLORS**
black, white, pink, and green

✂ **11 FELT PIECES**

2 rose hips x2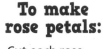

8 rose petals (cut in half) x8

1 rose petal bottom

🔄 **1 STEM**
half a pipe cleaner

MAKE A FACE

① Add a face to one of the rose hips. Set it aside for later.

To make rose petals:

Cut each rose circle in half to make 16 petals.

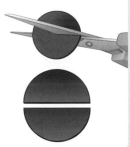

SEW TOGETHER

② Stack two petals on top of each other. Lay the top petal halfway across the bottom petal.

③ With a threaded needle, poke through the spot where the petals overlap and make a stitch.

④ Continue stacking the petals, following Steps 2–3, until you have a rose petal chain. Finish it with an ending knot.

The chain should look like this:

⑤ Starting at one end, begin rolling up the chain like a cinnamon bun.

⑥ Stop when you've rolled up half of the chain. Poke a threaded needle through the side of the rolled layers and out the bottom of the center a few times.

⑦ Roll up the rest of the chain and repeat Step 6 on the outer petals. Make sure the roll is secure, then make an ending knot.

Slow Your Roll!
Don't make an end knot quite yet. These halfway stitches keep the roll together.

⑧ Add the rose bottom. Poke from the bottom and out through the center of the rose, then back down. Repeat until it's secure and finish it with an ending knot.

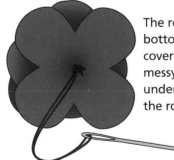

The rose bottom covers all the messy stitches underneath the rose!

Set the petals aside for now.

Try different colored petals to make a special rose.

OMBRÉ ROSE Sew the petals from darkest color to lightest.

Roll from this end. →

WILD ROSE
Sew two different-colored petals in a random order.

... Or try three different colors.

RAINBOW ROSE Sew the petals in the order of a rainbow.

Roll from this end. →

ADD A ROSE STEM

This stem attaches to the rose differently from the other flowers.

Cut the Stem
Fold a pipe cleaner in half and cut it with fingernail clippers.

9 Fold the end of the pipe cleaner down.

10 Stack the face on the other rose hip, with wrong sides facing each other. Whip stitch down the side, and place the folded end of the pipe cleaner between the pieces.

11 Keep stitching the rose hip, stopping when you get to the top.

12 Add stuffing to the rose hip. Leave a little space at the top of the cup.

13 With a threaded needle, poke from the inside of the rose hip. Place the rose on top, and stitch through the base of the petals.

14 Stitch around the entire rose hip, stitching through the petals as you go. Finish it with an ending knot.

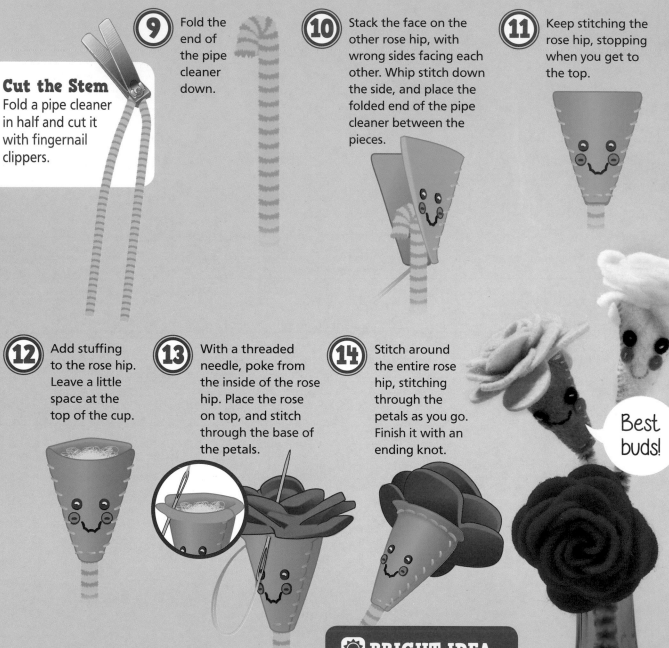

Best buds!

☼ BRIGHT IDEA
You can gently pull back the petals to help shape the rose!

GNOME

MAKE A FACE

1 Place the head piece on one body. Then attach it with a straight stitch down both sides of the head.

2 Stack the beard on the face. Then stitch each side of the beard in place.

3 Sew eyes on the face, and a mouth on the beard. Use an extra cheek to make a nose.

MAKE A HAT

4 Whip stitch the two straight edges of the hat to make a cone. Finish it with an ending knot.

5 Pop the hat open. The seam will be the back of the hat.

SEW TOGETHER

6 Stack the two body pieces, wrong sides together. Whip stitch around the sides, leaving the bottom open.

7 Stuff, then whip stitch the bottom closed. Finish with an ending knot.

Place the hat on top of the gnome. Adjust how he wants to wear it, then add a stitch in the back to secure.

GARDEN GUIDE

❀ **FLOWER FRIEND**

⊘ **5 FLOSS COLORS**
black, white, pink, red, and yellow

✂ **5 FELT PIECES**

1 gnome hat

x2 — 2 gnome bodies

1 gnome head

1 gnome beard

● 1 nose (use a pink cheek or a small scrap of pink felt)

51

BUTTERFLY

Poke a thin wire or an unfolded paper clip from home through the body to make the butterfly flutter.

GARDEN GUIDE

🌼 **FLOWER FRIEND**

🧵 **3 FLOSS COLORS**
black, white, and purple

✂️ **3 FELT PIECES**

x2
2 butterfly bodies

1 butterfly wings

MAKE A FACE

1 Add a face to one of the butterfly bodies.

MAKE WINGS

2 Decorate the butterfly wings, or skip to Step 3 if you want them plain.

WING TIP

- Use a floss color that pops against the felt.
- Use a pencil or light-colored pen to draw a design on the wings before stitching.

Get creative with your sewing skills:
- Back stitch to make polka dots.
- Straight stitch to make lines.
- Whip stitch around the edge of the wings.

3 Lay the wings on top of the plain butterfly body, wrong side up, so they lie right under the head.

4 Sew down the middle of the wings, through the body. Finish it with an ending knot (page 15).

SEW TOGETHER

5 Place the body with a face on top. Whip stitch the pieces together, leaving a small gap at the bottom.

6 Stuff the body and whip stitch the gap closed. Finish it with an ending knot.

Stitch the butterfly to the stem of a flower to make it look like it's sitting pretty.